MW01275493

R·O·M·A·N·S

IDENTITY in CHRIST

DR. ROB GODARD

Copyright © 2019 Cloverdale Baptist Church
All rights reserved
Cover & book design by Elias Cabrera
ISBN: 9781794374881

DEDICATION

Romans is a book that has impacted my life more than any other. Its depth, breadth, and call to trust in God no matter what, has enriched my experience of God's love unlike any other book. Romans is a book we could live in and never tire of. I am thankful for my family that serves with me and reaps the benefits and pains of being related to a servant of the church, as a servant of her LORD. Thank you, Lori, for longing to grow in your love for Jesus and help your children do the same. Thank you Ryan, Jeff, Ben and Graeme for being willing to share our family with the church, and to hear your stories shared on Sundays (okay $5 helped) with joy. I love you, and am proud to have you as my family through all of the ups and downs that we have experienced and will experience on this journey together. Thank you! My greatest hope for our family is that we would live victorious lives in Christ, and this part of Romans communicates this in a way that, if understood and internalized, will change our lives!

A father's greatest joy is to have his children walking in the truth.

ACKNOWLEDGMENTS

It is exciting to serve God at Cloverdale Baptist Church. I am thankful for great elders and deacons, and a staff that seeks God-glorifying excellence. Judi, Pastor Les, and Elias, well done again on pushing for this to get done. It is good to serve Jesus together in this local church!

I love Jesus' church and am honoured to serve her!

TABLE OF CONTENTS

GROWTH GROUPS

This book is put together to help Growth Groups at Cloverdale Baptist Church effectively apply God's Word to everyday life. We want the Word of God not only to be preached, but applied, and one of the key ways of ensuring this reality is if we discuss what was shared on Sunday in a way that seeks to deepen the impact. Certainly we can do this with families and friends, however at CBC the programmed way we seek to maximize this impact is Growth Groups.

There are three reasons for making the development of these study books a priority at Cloverdale Baptist Church:

1. We want to prioritize the hearing and applying of God's Word.

This is essential for the authentication of who God's people are (Matthew 7:21-28) and our growth into being who God wants us to be (Psalm 138:2; James 1:22-25). It is our prayer and desire that this book helps you to focus on what God's Word is saying, and that it helps to lead you into applying His Word to everyday life.

2. We value small group ministry.

It is our belief that small group ministry can produce passion in God's people (Hebrews 10:25), and serve as a protection for God's people (Hebrews 3:12–14). Sin can be deceitful, and hardened hearts can lead to despair. Small group ministry protects us from sin, and engages our hearts for devotion. We would love for all our people to be engaged in small group ministry, grow to love one another, and God, more and more.

3. We are looking for long term change.

It is our hope, as we interact with God's Word together, that these books will help you remember what you are learning and longing to apply. It is our desire that they become for you a tool to look back at, and grow with in the coming years as you continue to progress in conformity to the image of our Lord Jesus (Galatians 4:19). We believe that God's Word is powerful and will not return void (Isaiah 55:11), and it is helpful for His people to have reminders of where He has equipped them for every good work (2 Timothy 3:16–17).

If you are not in a small group we encourage you to join one, and until you do, use the questions part of this notebook not only for reflection, but to interact with your family and/or friends in a way that is actively seeking to apply the Bible to your life (Deuteronomy 6:1–9). May our God use this book through the power of His Spirit to bring change in His people for His glory.

OVERVIEW

Perhaps no other letter in the history of the world has had such a tremendous impact as the book of Romans.

John MacArthur states, *"Most, if not all, of the great revivals and reformations in the history of the church have been directly related to the book of Romans... It's commonly agreed that the Epistle to the Romans is one of the greatest Christian writings. Its power has been demonstrated again and again at critical points in the history of the church."*

As I long for revival in my own life and in this church, Romans is one of the most powerful places to go to produce it in us.

Romans is written somewhere between 56–58 A.D.; Paul is in Corinth on his third missionary journey and longing to be a part of what is going on in the Roman church. The book is about life change as an overflow of experiencing the Gospel (1:5, 16–17). It draws us closer to God so we can without shame draw others in the same direction.

It is not a systematic theology, and yet the theology in the book of Romans is overwhelmingly rich, with each part adding to the whole and leaving every Spirit-filled believer overwhelmed with God's love. Romans is a book that changes the world by changing people. So, as we prayerfully engage in this journey together, may we offer ourselves afresh to God, to the impact of His Gospel and the glory of the message of this letter.

Oh that we would be revived in our passion and first love for God as we experience His love!

Romans: Book 2 covers many rich themes, and seeks to continue to drive home the Gospel in an applicable manner.

KEY WORDS & CONCEPTS IN ROMANS[1]

Condemnation: This is a word used in Romans to show God's right view of sinful humanity in their guilt before Him. It is what He views us as (condemned) in showing what we rightly deserve because of our sin and is the opposite of justification.

Faith: Hebrews 11:1, 6 describes it as being certain of what we hope for and certain of what we cannot see. It is also something that allows us to please God, and without it, it becomes impossible to please God. Perhaps simply understood, it is "the unqualified acceptance of and dependence on the completed work of Jesus Christ to secure God's mercy toward believers (Swindoll)". It is all of grace (Ephesians 2:1–10) and is essential for salvation and sanctification.

Flesh: As used in theology, it describes the identity of humans who are not saved by grace through faith and the orientation that believers battle after being saved. Those who belong to Jesus battle the flesh, the world, and the devil. The battle against the flesh is a battle against habits and patterns of thinking that are in opposition to God and are ultimately self-centred.

Glorification: This is the end of salvation. It will be the reality that all who die in Christ receive, most fully, when Jesus returns for His church. This will include an absolute freedom from sin and its consequences and a beauty in conformity to Christ in incorruptible perfect bodies that will last for all eternity in the presence of God.

Gospel: The word gospel simply means *"good news"*. When Christians use this term, they mean the good news about Jesus Christ.

This includes the holiness of God and His demand for perfection and the fallenness of humans and their sin that falls short of God's glory and the wonder of the life, death, burial, and resurrection of Jesus and the call to respond to this grace by faith in Jesus alone.

The Gospel is, broadly speaking, the entire Bible, but, simply, it is focused on Jesus and the cross.

A good summary of the Gospel from 9 Marks is:

1. *God.* God is the creator of all things (Gen. 1:1). He is perfectly holy, worthy of all worship, and will punish sin (1 John 1:5, Rev. 4:11, Rom. 2:5–8).

---

[1] Idea taken from Swindoll, Charles: Coming To Terms With Sin. IFL

2. *Man.* All people, though created good, have become sinful by nature (Gen. 1:26–28, Ps. 51:5, Rom. 3:23). From birth, all people are alienated from God, hostile to God, and subject to the wrath of God (Eph. 2:1–3).

3. *Christ.* Jesus Christ, who is fully God and fully man, lived a sinless life, died on the cross to bear God's wrath in the place of all who would believe in him, and rose from the grave in order to give his people eternal life (John 1:1, 1 Tim. 2:5, Heb. 7:26, Rom. 3:21–26, 2 Cor. 5:21, 1 Cor. 15:20–22).

4. *Response.* God calls everyone everywhere to repent of their sins and trust in Christ in order to be saved (Mark 1:15, Acts 20:21, Rom. 10:9–10).

(Some of this material has been adapted from The Gospel and Personal Evangelism by Mark Dever, p. 43) *https://www.9marks.org/answer/what-gospel/*

Grace: God's unmerited favour given to sinners who deserve His wrath and from Him receive good. Being saved by grace includes the reality that there is nothing in humans that could earn or cause them to deserve being saved, but God who is rich in grace chooses in that grace to save those who deserve wrath. Sometimes an acrostic for this has been used: *"God's Riches At Christ's Expense"*. It is good but leaves out the undeserved nature of this. Instead of receiving God's wrath and judgment, which all humans deserve, those who experience saving grace receive His love and blessing. Salvation is *all of grace*.

Justification: This is a precious word that some have defined as *"the declared reality for Christians that we are righteous—just as if I had never sinned"*, and that is helpful, but awesomely it is more; it includes *"just as if I had always obeyed"*. Swindoll helpfully defines it like this, *"God's declaration or pronouncement that sinners, upon believing in Christ, are righteous because of Christ—even though still in a sinning state."* Those who believe are *declared righteous*.

Propitiation: This is the satisfaction of God's wrath against sin through the shed blood of Jesus on the cross. For Christians it is the reality that God's wrath, rightly being poured out against sin and sinners, has been satisfied on their behalf by Jesus (2 Corinthians 5:21).

Regeneration: This word refers to rebirth, or being born again. Humans are born in sin, and are dead in their trespasses and sin. Spiritual birth results in regeneration and changes who the believer is. Christ is formed in their hearts, and they are made partakers in the divine nature (2 Corinthians 5:17).

Sanctification: The basic meaning of *"sanctify"*, is to be set apart. As this word is used, it is the pursuit of becoming who we are, or the pursuit of holiness. It is the process by which Christians move towards practical holiness. It is the growth process towards being like Jesus (Romans 8:29). God's Spirit works in His followers to will and to act as they discipline their lives for holiness.

Sin: Sin is anything that falls short of God's glory. It means to have missed the mark, and humans are sinful by nature, nurture, and choice. The condition that sin places humans under is called slavery, and freedom can only be found in Christ. It is a transgression of God's holy law and includes action and passivity. It places humans under God's righteous holy judgment as those born in sin who are slaves to sin and continue to sin.

Sovereignty: What does it mean that God is sovereign? It means that God is *all powerful, all knowing*, and *all wise* and is working everything out in conformity to the purpose of His Will (Ephesians 1:11). He is over all things and is the *Sovereign Ruler*.

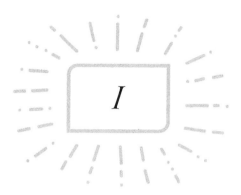

IDENTITY: ADAM OR JESUS

Romans 5:12–21

We live in a fallen world, and the spiritual explanation for this is the fall of humanity through the sin of Adam. This sin was on behalf of all humans, and brought with it death and separation from God. The only hope for those who are trapped in this sin by virtue of their being born human is the free gift of God through Jesus Christ. For us as humans we have only two options of identity—Adam or Christ. The way to receive the abundance of Jesus' perfect life and death in our place is to trust in Him so that grace may reign through righteousness leading to eternal life.

Sometimes as we come to this doctrine the logic is hard to follow, and perhaps even harder to apply. This passage means to drive us to praise God for His amazing grace, a grace that saved us from our identity of sin in Adam, to our identity of righteousness with Christ. This is an understanding that is truly life changing, and one that should lead to an overwhelming joy in the grace that has brought us forgiveness in Christ.

As we study this passage together, our prayer is that it will cause your heart to experience the overwhelming grace of God and the freedom that this brings to serve Him.

IDENTITY: ADAM OR JESUS

ROMANS 5:12–21

Introduction

1. How did we get here? | VERSES 12–14

2. How do we get out of here? | VERSES 15–21

Implications
• Know where we are

• Know where we could be

• Choose Jesus

• Rejoice & be ruled by grace

EXTRA NOTES

EXTRA NOTES

GROWTH GROUP QUESTIONS

ROMANS 5:12–21

• Who are you?

• Why is it important to answer this question in a theologically correct way?

• How does how we view ourselves matter to how we live our lives?

• How does the Bible paint a picture that shows that we are either identified with Christ, or with Adam?

• What does it mean that, *"in Adam, we all sinned"*?

• Discuss the doctrine of imputed sin (Psalm 51:5)? EPHESIANS 1:1–3

• Why is it important to understand and believe this doctrine?

• How does the Bible offer hope for humans who are born in sin, or as this text states, identified with Adam?

• Why is a proper understanding of grace essential to battle the sin we are born in and do?

• Ray Stedman states, *"All your life, as many times as you sin, you cannot out-sin the grace of God. No matter how many trespasses are involved in your record there is freedom in Christ and forgiveness for all of them."*

  > How can you live in light of this?

• Are you identified with Adam, or with Jesus?

• What does it mean to you personally to be identified *in* Jesus?

• Sometimes passages like this can get us bogged down in doctrine, rather than lifted up in praise. Take the time as you end this study to praise God for His grace! May this understanding of identity drive you to *confidence in Christ* and His grace!

EXTRA NOTES

EXTRA NOTES

PRAYER

Thank you for praying together as a small group. We believe that prayer together is essential to your health and our family's health.

For the next 10 weeks we want to focus our prayers together as a church meeting in small groups on revival.

> ### PSALM 85:6

"Will you not revive us again, that your people may rejoice in you?"

As you pray, we hope that the following outline will help you:

1. Praise God for who He is:
   - He is *holy holy holy*
   - He is faithful
   - He is gracious and compassionate, slow to anger and abounding in love

2. Thank God for what He has done:
   - Begin with your so *great salvation*
   - Thank Him for other good gifts He has given you
   - Thank Him for the privilege of being able to be on mission for Him

3. Requests you have as a group:

4. For revival | PSALM 85:6

Pray that God's people at Cloverdale, starting with you, will have a new love for God's Word.

MEMORIZE
& MEDITATE

"Will you not revive us again, that your people may rejoice in you?"

PSALM 85:6

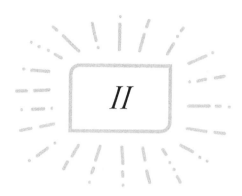

MAY IT NEVER BE

Romans 6:1–2

When the Gospel is understood in the richness of the grace of God, often there is a temptation to sin, in light of God's grace. Romans 6 shows us that true identity with Jesus means a new life of obedience to Him. You cannot truly know Him, or experience the richness of His grace without being one who seeks to obey Him. This does not mean that we will not struggle, or that we will all of a sudden be perfect. It does mean that our freedom in Jesus will lead us to follow Him.

James Montgomery Boice has called Romans 6:2 the most important verse in the Bible for the modern Christian, and although I would include many others in this discussion, it is essential that as Canadians we recognize that identity in Christ, being objects of His amazing grace, not only frees us from condemnation, it moves us to a life that will be lived in the freedom of slavery to Jesus.

As we work our way through this amazing chapter, take the time to read all of chapter 6 each week so that the richness of the greater context is not lost as we enjoy the treasure of each verse. My prayer as we study verses 1–2 is that we would rejoice in grace, grasp its overwhelming richness and walk in newness of life.

 MAY IT NEVER BE

ROMANS 6:1–2

Introduction

1. Interest in staying slaves | VERSE 1

2. The pathway of rejection | VERSE 2

- Romans 5:21
- Ephesians 5:5
- 1 Cor. 6:9–11
- 1 John 3:9–10
- Titus 2:11–13
- 2 Cor. 5:17
- James 2:14
- Philippians 1:6

Implications

- We died to sin. How can we live in it any longer?

- Live life free, for the glory of God!

EXTRA NOTES

EXTRA NOTES

GROWTH GROUP QUESTIONS

ROMANS 6:1–2

- Spend time as a group defining grace, using words that express the meaning we have given, but are more personally defined.

  > Grace is God's riches at Christ's expense.

  > Grace is getting more than I deserve.

  > Grace is God's free unmerited favor given to sinners who deserve only wrath.

- Why do you think the Bible presents grace in such a way that there is a danger it could be misunderstood and lead to people thinking that they should sin to make grace abound?

- How can we present God's grace in this same way?

- How can we help people fight against the temptation to live however they want because of the richness of God's grace?

- Is it okay for a Christian to treat sin in their life lightly?

• How is it impossible for a true Christian to think this way? MATTHEW 7:21–27

• Interact with James Montgomery Boice's quote, *"to understand this statement is to understand how to live a holy life. And because it is the key to sanctification I would go so far as to say that Romans 6:2 is the most important verse in the Bible for believers in evangelical churches to understand today"*.

> Do you agree? Disagree? Why?

> Why do you think that he said this?

• Read the following Scriptures and discuss what each means, and why it fits with the passage we are studying.

  • Romans 5:21
  • Ephesians 5:5
  • 1 Corinthians 6:9–11
  • 1 John 3:9–10
  • Titus 2:11–13
  • 2 Corinthians 5:17
  • James 2:14
  • Philippians 1:6

• How can we show ourselves to be those who have died to sin?

EXTRA NOTES

EXTRA NOTES

PRAYER

Thank you for praying together as a small group. We believe that prayer together is essential to your health and our family's health.

For the next 10 weeks we want to focus our prayers together as a church meeting in small groups on revival.

> PSALM 85:6

"Will you not revive us again, that your people may rejoice in you?"

As you pray, we hope that the following outline will help you:

1. Praise God for who He is:
   - God is all powerful
   - God is good
   - God is all wise

2. Thank God for what He has done:
   - Begin with your *so great salvation*
   - Thank Him for other good gifts He has given you
   - Thank Him for the privilege of being able to be on mission for Him

3. Requests you have as a group:

4. For revival:

*"If my people who are called by my name **humble themselves**, and pray and seek my face and turn from their wicked ways, then I will hear from heaven and will forgive their sin and heal their land."* 2 Chronicles 7:14

Pray that we would be a people at Cloverdale Baptist who are authentic in our salvation. That we would be Gospel-centred and saturated, knowing we are called by His name. That we would acknowledge that He owns us and we are His people!

"By no means! How can we who died to sin still live in it?"

ROMANS 6:2

DEAD MEN WALKING

Romans 6:3–14

This passage is one of the richest in the Bible on what it means to identify with Jesus so intimately that we are found in Him. This identity when understood and experienced will change how we live.

False religion over the years has slipped off of the Biblical highway into the ditch, one side of the ditch that we must earn our salvation, and the other that there is no newness of life for those in Christ. When we grasp our identity in Jesus we will stay on the road and avoid the ditches. Understanding that we died with Christ means we can experience true forgiveness, we can be dead to the rule of sin, and live for God as those found in Him.

Baptism pictures so beautifully what Jesus has done for us on the cross, and what we have done with Him in being crucified and raised to life (Galatians 2:20). Now we can live as those who literally clothe ourselves with Christ (Galatians 3:27).

This is a passage that focuses on the results of the Gospel and helps us to be those who never lose sight of this good news. May God help us to experience the richness of what He has done so that we live for His glory with every breath we take. May we find new life, new passion, new freedom in our identity with Jesus!

DEAD MEN WALKING

ROMANS 6:3–14

Introduction

1. You died with Christ

GALATIANS 2:20

2. You were raised with Christ

2 CORINTHIANS 5:17   EPHESIANS 2:1–10

Boice states, *"The secret of sanctification is not some neat set of experiences or emotions, however meaningful or intense they may be. It is knowing what has happened to you."*

3. Walk in newness of life in Christ

COLOSSIANS 3:1   1 CORINTHIANS 6:15   GENESIS 3:27   GALATIANS 2:20

Implications

• Focus on the reality of the gospel

• Foundational gospel truths

• Fully identify with Jesus

• Fill the tank

EXTRA NOTES

EXTRA NOTES

GROWTH GROUP QUESTIONS

ROMANS 6:3–14

- How does the story of Martin Luther help us to grasp the need we have to experience grace?

- Why is it helpful for us to understand history, especially Christian history?

- Why was the Reformation needed?

- Discuss together what you know about the Reformation.

- Where do you think the church today in Canada needs a reformation?

- What does it mean that we died with Christ?

- Why is this reality important to be aware of and to experience?

- How does this reality help you to experience forgiveness?

- What does it mean to be dead to the rule of sin?

- Discuss the reality of Galatians 2:20

- What does it mean to be raised with Christ?

- Why is this reality important to be aware of and experience?

- How does knowing what has happened to us in Christ help us to walk in newness of life?

- What does a healthy life in Christ look like?

- Discuss how Colossians 3:15 and 1 Corinthians 6:15 help us to understand what it means to live our lives for God?

- What does it mean to *"put on Christ"*? GALATIANS 3:27

- How can you work individually and together as a group to apply the implications?
  - > Focus on the reality of the gospel
  - > Foundational gospel truths for new life
  - > Full identify with Jesus
  - > Fill the tank

EXTRA NOTES

EXTRA NOTES

PRAYER

Thank you for praying together as a small group. We believe that prayer together is essential to your health and our family's health.

For the next 10 weeks we want to focus our prayers together as a church meeting in small groups on revival.

> **PSALM 85:6**

"Will you not revive us again, that your people may rejoice in you?"

As you pray, we hope that the following outline will help you:

1. Praise God for who He is:
   - He is righteous
   - He is merciful
   - He is just

2. Thank God for what He has done:
   - Begin with your *so great salvation*
   - Thank Him for other good gifts He has given you
   - Thank Him for the privilege of being able to be on mission for Him

3. Requests you have as a group:

4. For revival:

"If my people who are called by my name humble themselves, and pray and seek my face and turn from their wicked ways, then I will hear from heaven and will forgive their sin and heal their land." 2 Chronicles 7:14

Pray that we at Cloverdale Baptist Church (remember revival begins with you) would be those who are humble before God. That we would see how awesome He is, and in that see ourselves in light of His greatness!

MEMORIZE
& MEDITATE

"So you also must consider yourselves dead to sin and alive to God in Christ Jesus."

ROMANS 6:11

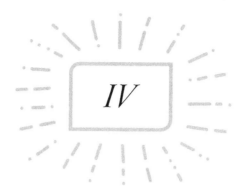

IDENTITY CRISIS SOLVED

Romans 6:3–14

When you are introducing yourself, how do you do it? Usually we tie our identity to what we do. When I played a lot of hockey, and my college days were coming to an end, an older friend took me aside and shared that for him, when hockey ended it was a time of identity crisis. How we see ourselves actually makes a large difference in terms of how we live our lives. For those who are in Christ, this identity is to become what most defines us in how we think of ourselves, and in how we live.

Galatians 2:20 powerfully sums it up in one verse, *"I have been crucified with Christ. It is no longer I who live, but Christ who lives in me. And the life I now live in the flesh I live by faith in the Son of God, who loved me and gave himself for me."*

My longing for us as a church is that not only would we be able to know and say that we are in Christ, we would understand it well enough to live in light of it, this life of faith in Jesus. Romans is moving forward in describing the *power of the gospel* and showing that it not only saves those who don't deserve it, by grace through faith, but also that this fundamentally changes who we are, thus how we should see ourselves, and ultimately how we live.

I am in Christ!

IDENTITY CRISIS SOLVED

ROMANS 6:3–14

Introduction

1. Who am I? I am in Christ

GALATIANS 2:20	COLOSSIANS 3:3

Crucified with Christ
Christ lives in me
I now live by faith
in the Son of God
who loved me and gave
himself for me

You died, your life is now hidden with Christ in God

2. How do I get in Christ? By grace through faith

2 TIMOTHY 1:9	EPHESIANS 1:4	1 CORINTHIANS 12:13

Do not be ashamed to
testify about our Lord or
ashamed of me his prisoner.
But join me in suffering for
the gospel by the power of God
who has saved us and called
us to a holy life — Not by anything we have
done but because of His
purpose and grace. This
grace was given us in Christ
Jesus before the beginning
of time
I am not ashamed because
I know whom I believed
and am convinced that He
is able to guard what I have
entrusted to Him to that day

He chose us in
Him before the
creation of the
world to be holy
and blameless in
his sight.

We were all baptized
by one Spirit into one
body — and were
all given the one Spirit
to drink.

3. What does it mean to be in Christ? Transformative *God made Him who had no sin to be sin for us, so that in Him we might become the Righteousness of God*
  - I am Righteous in Christ: 2 Corinthians 5:21
  - I am Free in Christ: Romans 6:6–7 *No longer slave to sin*
  - I am in Fellowship with Christ: Romans 6:3,4 *Buried with Him through baptism into death in order that we too may live a new life*
  - I am a New Creation In Christ: 2 Corinthians 5:17 ✓
  - I am in Battle: Romans 6:11–14 *Do's + don'ts*
  - I have a Guaranteed Future: Romans 6:9
  - I have Peace: Philippians 4:7, 19

4. Why does this matter? Worldview

5. When am I in Christ? Conversion

6. How does this make a difference in my life today? Everything changes!

EXTRA NOTES

EXTRA NOTES

GROWTH GROUP QUESTIONS

ROMANS 6:3–14

- How does your view of yourself impact how you live?

- Why is it so important to god that we see ourselves in Christ?

- What does it mean to be in Christ?

- How does someone get in Christ?

- Why does this matter?

- Review the meaning of Pastor Rob's focus on Sunday of what it means to be in Christ.

• Interact on each to makes sure you have an understanding of what each means and how each applies to life.

> I am Righteous in Christ: 2 Corinthians 5:21

> I am Free in Christ: Romans 6:6–7

> I am in Fellowship with Christ: Romans 6:3

> I am a New Creation In Christ: 2 Corinthians 5:17

> I am in Battle: Romans 6:11–14

> I have a Guaranteed Future: Romans 6:9

> I have Peace: Philippians 4:7, 19

• How do these specific things change how you live your life?

• Why does God's Word spend so much time on our identity in Christ?

• How can you show your true identity to those around you?

EXTRA NOTES

EXTRA NOTES

PRAYER

Thank you for praying together as a small group. We believe that prayer together is essential to your health and our family's health.

For the next 10 weeks we want to focus our prayers together as a church meeting in small groups on revival.

> **PSALM 85:6**

"Will you not revive us again, that your people may rejoice in you?"

As you pray, we hope that the following outline will help you:

1. Praise God for who He is:
   - God is love
   - God never changes
   - God is jealous

2. Thank God for what He has done:
   - Begin with your *so great salvation*
   - Thank Him for other good gifts He has given you
   - Thank Him for the privilege of being able to be on mission for Him

3. Requests you have as a group:

4. For revival:
*"If my people who are called by my name **humble themselves**, and pray and seek my face and turn from their wicked ways, then I will hear from heaven and will forgive their sin and heal their land."* **2 Chronicles 7:14**

- Pray that we would be a people who are actively dependent on God and that more and more we would show this spirit of dependence by our commitment to praying together and alone.

MEMORIZE
& MEDITATE

"I have been crucified with Christ. It is no longer I who live, but Christ who lives in me. And the life I now live in the flesh I live by faith in the Son of God, who loved me and gave himself for me."

GALATIANS 2:20

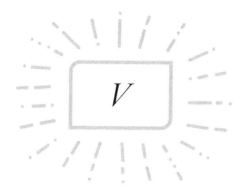

LEARNING TO COUNT

Romans 6:15–23

How we think impacts how we live. This is not only something that people in this generation assume through books like *"I'm okay, you're okay"* but way more importantly from God's Word. If we can learn to take captive every thought, and reckon, or count ourselves dead and alive, our lives will conform more willingly to Jesus. To do this is a choice, it is a disciplined pursuit, and something that every believer must learn to do if they are to find victory in their battle for holiness in a hurting world.

The reality of Christianity is most impactful on Christians when they learn that reality impacts life. Count yourselves dead to sin and alive to Christ!

 **LEARNING TO COUNT**

ROMANS 6:15–23

Introduction

1. Count yourselves dead and alive
   • No fear in temptation

   • No fear of death

   • Know peace in His presence

2. Count on your life as belonging to God

  • Count your mind as His

  • Count your eyes and ears as His

  • Count your tongue as His

  • Count your hands and feet as His

Implications

EXTRA NOTES

EXTRA NOTES

GROWTH GROUP QUESTIONS

ROMANS 6:15–23

• If anyone in your group has travelled to Israel share your highlight of the trip.

• If no one has, or if you want to keep sharing, for those who haven't, what would you love to see?

• Why did Jesus let Lazarus die?'

• How does the story of Lazarus help us to understand our salvation?

• Why is our pursuit of holiness as Christians so important?

• What does it mean to count ourselves dead and alive?

• How can you do this? Make sure to be practical in your answers.

- How does this help us to not fear temptation? Death?

- How does this help us to experience peace?

- What does it mean that you belong to God?

- Why is what we do with our minds so important to this pursuit of holiness?
    > Romans 12:1–2
    > Colossians 3:1–4
    > Philippians 4:8

- What does it mean to count your eyes and ears as His?

- What does it mean to count your tongue as His? JAMES 3:3–8

- What does it meant to count your hands and feet as His?

- How can you use this text to help you push forward in your desire to pursue holiness?

EXTRA NOTES

EXTRA NOTES

PRAYER

Thank you for praying together as a small group. We believe that prayer together is essential to your health and our family's health.

For the next 10 weeks we want to focus our prayers together as a church meeting in small groups on revival.

PSALM 85:6

"Will you not revive us again, that your people may rejoice in you?"

As you pray, we hope that the following outline will help you:

1. Praise God for who He is:
   - God is gracious
   - God is eternal
   - God is self-sufficient

2. Thank God for what He has done:
   - Begin with your *so great salvation*
   - Thank Him for other good gifts He has given you
   - Thank Him for the privilege of being able to be on mission for Him

3. Requests you have as a group:

4. For revival:

"If my people who are called by my name humble themselves, and pray and seek my face and turn from their wicked ways, then I will hear from heaven and will forgive their sin and heal their land." 2 Chronicles 7:14

Pray that we truly would seek the face of God. That we would long for intimacy with Him, and in this seek to live in a way that brings Him glory! We seek His face when we study His Word to sharpen our view of Him! Long to know Him as He has revealed Himself!

MEMORIZE
& MEDITATE

"For the wages of sin is death, but the free gift of God is eternal life in Christ Jesus our Lord."

ROMANS 6:23

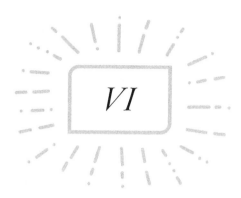

CALLED FROM SLAVERY TO SLAVERY

Romans 6:15–23

I hate slavery! Being a part of The Gospel Coalition and interacting with spiritual brothers who are still suffering the consequences of American slavery has left my heart broken and hating. So when the Bible uses this term, slavery, as a mark of those who follow Jesus it is a shock. In fact some scholars say that this is the number one word (*doulos*) that is used for those who have experienced the grace of God, and found freedom from sin in Christ.

Romans 6 is one of the great passages in the Bible that declares our identity in Christ, and displays our relationship to Him as our LORD. There is a freedom that comes from sin, and calls to obedience. This freedom is one that always leads to following, so that the great privilege of those freed, is to follow as slaves of Jesus.

He is a good and great Master, and this relationship, when understood, will yield holy lives that produces fruit, and have the delight of spending eternity in Christ Jesus our Lord. This passage discusses our freedom in Christ as a freedom for Christ, and is one every healthy believer must have as a core part of who they are. You are set free from sin, to obedience that leads to righteousness. As such, present yourselves to God, and follow Him!

CALLED FROM SLAVERY TO SLAVERY

ROMANS 6:15–23

Introduction

Everyone is a slave

JEREMIAH 2:11–13

• Sin is a horrible master

• Sin shames its subjects

• Sin has deadly consequences

Ray Stedman says, *"Death is both physical and moral; the one is a picture of the other. Physical death always involves darkness, the end of light and life. It involves limitation, for a corpse is helpless—what can it do for itself? And it involves ultimately, corruption— the corpse begins to stink and smell, it becomes foul and decayed, rottenness sets it."*

Implications

• Choose the right Master

• Choose to be set free

• Choose to present your bodies to God

EXTRA NOTES

EXTRA NOTES

GROWTH GROUP QUESTIONS

ROMANS 6:15–23

- Respond to the title of the sermon, *"called from slavery, to slavery"*.

- Do you agree that the #1 metaphor for the believer is a *"slave"*, of God?

- Why do you think we struggle with this language?

- Read Romans 6:15–23. How does this text teach that everyone is a slave?

- Interact with Kent Hughes, *"all humanity serves under one of two slaveries, either sin which leads to death, or obedience which leads to righteousness."*

- Read John 8:33. What does Jesus mean?

- How does sin display that it is a horrible master?

• In what way does sin shame its subjects?

• What are the consequences of sin?

• Read Jeremiah 2:12–13. What are the two options given to God's people?

• How can we *"choose the right Master"*?

• What does it mean to *"choose to be set free"* if we are called to follow Jesus as our LORD no matter what the cost?

• How can we present our bodies to God, as those who belong to Him?
1 CORINTHIANS 6:19–20

• How does the way that Jesus closes the Sermon on the Mount (Matthew 7:21–27) help us to grasp what being a slave of God looks like?

• Reflect on your own life, and ask God to search you, and to see if there is any area of your life that you need to become obedient to Him from the heart?

EXTRA NOTES

EXTRA NOTES

PRAYER

Thank you for praying together as a small group. We believe that prayer together is essential to your health and our family's health.

For the next 10 weeks we want to focus our prayers together as a church meeting in small groups on revival.

PSALM 85:6

"Will you not revive us again, that your people may rejoice in you?"

As you pray, we hope that the following outline will help you:

1. Praise God for who He is:

   Have each person share an attribute of God they are thankful for and why. Direct your conversation to God, as you praise Him, and rejoice in how He has revealed Himself to us.

2. Thank God for what He has done:
   - Begin with your *so great salvation*
   - Thank Him for other good gifts He has given you
   - Thank Him for the privilege of being able to be on mission for Him

3. Requests you have as a group:

4. For revival:

*"If my people who are called by my name **humble themselves**, and pray and seek my face and turn from their wicked ways, then I will hear from heaven and will forgive their sin and heal their land."* **2 Chronicles 7:14**

Pray that we would know what our wicked ways are (as the Bible defines them) and that we would turn from them.

Take time to confess your sins, and rejoice in the goodness of God's forgiveness.

1 JOHN 1:9; ROMANS 8:1

MEMORIZE & MEDITATE

"But now that you have been set free from sin and have become slaves of God, the fruit you get leads to sanctification and its end, eternal life."

ROMANS 6:22

FREEDOM ILLUSTRATED: GOD'S VIEW OF MARRIAGE

Romans 7:1–6

Marriage is one of the most beautiful God-given gifts in the world today. Marriage is His idea, and it is a creation ordinance for all humans to enjoy. Unfortunately, the fall has marred the purpose and permanence of marriage.

In our text, Paul uses God's view of marriage to help us to understand our relationship as followers of Jesus with the law. We are free from the consequences of disobeying the law because we have died in Jesus and therefore we now belong to Him, and will seek to bear fruit for Him.

Our culture has devalued marriage to the point where Paul's point is hard for us to hear, so this Sunday we are going to review what the Bible teaches about the purpose and permanence of marriage (won't spend a lot of time in Ephesians 5:22ff), and hope this journey will help us to re-establish our biblical view of marriage. This gift from God is to be enjoyed, and will only be enjoyed if understood and experienced from a Biblical experience.

May God use this text to help His followers know how serious and superb marriage is, and to ensure in our own lives and marriages we are displaying our commitment to Him and His Word.

✝ FREEDOM ILLUSTRATED: GOD'S VIEW OF MARRIAGE

ROMANS 7:1–6

Introduction

1. To be a Christian is to be married to Christ

2. To be a Christian is to honour marriage: God's way

- How does the Old Testament value marriage?
  DEUTERONOMY 24:1–4 | MALACHI 2:13–16

Matthew 19:3–9
- Marriage is ordained by God at Creation
- God joins people in marriage
- God expects what He has joined to not be separated

- What is marital unfaithfulness?

- Can you get remarried if you are the innocent party?

Implications
- Jesus wants us to be a people who relationally make Him our priority

- Jesus uses marriage as a picture

- Jesus is gracious

EXTRA NOTES

EXTRA NOTES

GROWTH GROUP QUESTIONS

ROMANS 7:1–6

- Read Romans 7:1–4

- How do you think the culture views marriage in our world today?

- Why do you think the culture seems to fight against what God has revealed marriage is to be in His Word?

- What does Paul use marriage as an illustration of?

- What does it mean to be married to Christ?

- How can we show this as individuals, and in how we value His bride, as seen in the local church?

- What does it mean to honour marriage?

- Why do you think the Bible is against divorce?

MATTHEW 5:31–32 | ROMANS 7:1–4 | MALACHI 2:16 | MATTHEW 19:3–9

- How does understanding marriage as a creation ordinance help us in thinking through this subject?

- What does it mean that God joins people together when they are married?

- What are the two reasons that someone can be biblically remarried?

- How can we be a church that loves and provides healing for those broken by the consequences of divorce and still take a biblical position on this issue?

- Read Ephesians 5:22–32
- What is the picture that marriage is supposed to display?

- How can we pursue this in our relationship with God and one another?

- What should be our role in defending a biblical view of marriage in the church? In the culture?

EXTRA NOTES

EXTRA NOTES

PRAYER

Thank you for praying together as a small group. We believe that prayer together is essential to your health and our family's health.

PSALM 85:6

"Will you not revive us again, that your people may rejoice in you?"

As you pray, we hope that the following outline will help you. Discuss these together so that you are praising and thanking focused on the truth of who God is and what He has done.

1. Praise God for who He is:

   Have each person share an attribute of God they are thankful for and why. Direct your conversation to God, as you praise Him, and rejoice in how He has revealed Himself to us.

2. Thank God for what He has done:
   - Begin with your *so great salvation*
   - Thank Him for other good gifts He has given you
   - Thank Him for the privilege of being able to be on mission for Him

3. Requests you have as a group:

4. For revival:

"If my people who are called by my name humble themselves, and pray and seek my face and turn from their wicked ways, then I will hear from heaven and will forgive their sin and heal their land." **2 Chronicles 7:14**

Pray with faith...this is a promised response from God when the life and prayers of His people match this text. 2 Chronicles is given directly to God's people Israel, but indirectly we can see how He works, and boldly ask Him for Revival.

Ask God for **revival**, starting each individual praying, then to the group, then to our church, and then to our nation. Pray with confidence, for if our hearts have truly responded to God's Word, we can be confident that He has heard us and will do what is best in us and through us. Offer yourself fully to God!

MEMORIZE
& MEDITATE

"This mystery is profound, and I am saying that it refers to Christ and the church."

EPHESIANS 5:32

FREEDOM TO FOLLOW

Romans 7:1–6

We often struggle understanding the power of being freed from the law, through being in Christ. However all of us know what it means to struggle with our own sin, and self-worth, and this text frees us to be those who can walk in the Spirit, in obedience to our Lord Jesus and live our lives for Him.

Understanding these verses will free us from the guilt of not being able to obey the law in its entirety in a way that allows us to see ourselves in Christ, and yields a passion for obedience to Him. The better we grasp the purpose of the law and cling to Jesus the more we will seek to see our lives be filled with fruit for His glory.

My prayer is that through our study of this passage we will experience freedom, and slavery in a way that leaves us filled with joy, and full devotion to our Master.

✝ FREEDOM TO FOLLOW

ROMANS 7:1–6

Introduction

1. The law is binding only on the living

2. Through Christ you are dead

ROMANS 6:1–7   PSALM 119:97

- Legalism

- Antinomianism

3. You belong to Jesus

MATTHEW 7:21–27   ROMANS 1:5   2 COR 5:14–15

Implications

• Bear fruit for God

    > Character/Impact/Praise/Speech

• Serve in the Spirit

• Live for Him

EXTRA NOTES

EXTRA NOTES

GROWTH GROUP QUESTIONS

ROMANS 7:1–6

- How does the law help us to know Jesus better?

- Respond to Keller's quote, *"you can be either married to the law, or married to Christ, but you cannot be unmarried"*.

- How is the law only binding on the living?

- Why is this such an important point for Paul to make for the readers of this letter in the first century? For us?

- What does it mean that we are dead to the law through Christ?

- What is legalism?

- How do people use a false sense of legalism to pursue sin and avoid moral purity?

- What is antinomianism?

- How do people use this to pursue legalism?

- How can you as an individual avoid both ditches (legalism and antinomianism) and stay focused on relationship with Jesus and the Gospel?

- How can we be those who love the law, and yet have been freed from its bondage? PSALM 119:97

- What does it mean to, *"belong to Jesus"*? 1 CORINTHIANS 6:19–20

- How do we show our allegiance to Jesus? MATTHEW 7:21–27 ROMANS 1:5

- What is spiritual fruit, and how can we produce it as those who have died with Jesus to the law?

- What does it mean to serve in the Spirit and how can you do this?

- What are steps you can take this week to live for Jesus?

EXTRA NOTES

EXTRA NOTES

PRAYER

Thank you for praying together as a small group. We believe that prayer together is essential to your health and our family's health.

PSALM 85:6

"Will you not revive us again, that your people may rejoice in you?"

As you pray, we hope that the following outline will help you. Discuss these together so that you are praising and thanking focused on the truth of who God is and what He has done.

1. Praise God for who He is:

    Have each person share an attribute of God they are thankful for and why. Direct your conversation to God, as you praise Him, and rejoice in how He has revealed Himself to us.

2. Thank God for what He has done:
    - Begin with your *so great salvation*.
    - Thank Him for other good gifts He has given you
    - Thank Him for the privilege of being able to be on mission for Him

3. Requests you have as a group:
    - Pray for your children. If you don't have children, for the youth of our church, and any in your group that do have children. Also pray for parents who are seeking to disciple their children through these next stages.

4. For revival:

"The law of the LORD is perfect, reviving the soul; the testimony of the LORD is sure, making wise the simple." Psalm 19:7

Pray that we would be loyal to God's Word, and love it as He does. That our devotion to Him would show in our time in the Word, and that as a church we would remain faithful, no matter what the cost.

Pray that we would know and apply God's Word to our lives.
Psalm 138:2; Isaiah 66:2

MEMORIZE & MEDITATE

"For the love of Christ controls us, because we have concluded this: that one has died for all, therefore all have died; [15] and he died for all, that those who live might no longer live for themselves but for him who for their sake died and was raised."

2 CORINTHIANS 5:14–15

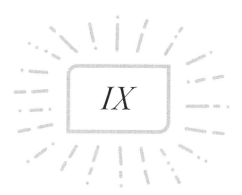

THE STRUGGLE AGAINST SIN IS REAL

Romans 7:7–25

One of the great tragedies the Canadian church faces is that we don't know how to fight sin, or perhaps worse, don't care if we fight sin or not. This is something that authentic Christians will avoid like the plague that it is.

While we are on earth, we will fight against sin in our own lives, heartbroken that we let Jesus down, and longing for holiness and purity in every area of our lives. Paul describes this battle in these verses and drives us to hope in the Gospel.

If you have ever felt overwhelmed at the greatness of your sin, and close to despair at the depth of your struggle, this passage breathes hope into the battle. Take heart, you are righteous in Christ, even as you are becoming righteous! Take heart, get your mind onto Jesus, and *rejoice* in great thanksgiving as you battle forward for God's glory.

THE STRUGGLE AGAINST SIN IS REAL

ROMANS 7:7–25

Introduction

Views on this passage | 1 TIMOTHY 1:15

- Before
- Carnal
- Conviction
- Mature Christian

1. The value of the law

HEBREWS 12:5–7

2. The victorious Christian life

How to battle sin in the life of the believer

S: Stay aware of sin in your life

I: Intentionally relate to God in grace and dependence

N: Never give up

- 1 Corinthians 9:24–27
- Ephesians 6:10–12
- Philippians 3:12–14
- Hebrews 12:1–4

EXTRA NOTES

EXTRA NOTES

GROWTH GROUP QUESTIONS

ROMANS 7:7–25

- We live in a world that pretends that sin does not exists. This is dangerous for many reasons, but two that rise to the top:

    1. People don't know what they need to be saved from, so conversion is surface and often false.

    2. Christians avoid the struggle with sin, slipping into apathy (no one can do this, so who cares), or legalism (fake it till you make it, and condemn everyone else).

- How can we avoid these two dangers as a church, as a growth group, and as individuals?

- Romans 7:7–25 has created a lot of controversy over the history of the church. Discuss the four options that Pastor Rob presented, and which one we think is right.

- How does this passage show us the value of the law?

- How can we learn to value the law this way?

- What does it mean to live the victorious Christian life in the midst of the struggle we all have with sin?

- Pastor Rob stated that we need to battle sin, and the way to do it. Discuss each of these, and how you can effectively choose to fight sin in your life through these three pathways.

  > **S** stay aware of sin in your life

  > **I** intentionally relate to God in grace and dependence

  > **N** never give up

- Why is fighting for holiness, and against sin so important for the believer?

- It was stated in the sermon that if we don't learn to understand this chapter in its biblical context we will live our lives in: despair, damning others, dispiritedness. Have you struggled with any of these?

- How can you help others who are struggling with these?

- What does it mean to preach the Gospel to yourself, and how can you do this every day, so as to fight sin, for holiness, in a way that is encouraged and centred on Jesus?

EXTRA NOTES

EXTRA NOTES

PRAYER

Thank you for praying together as a small group. We believe that prayer together is essential to your health and our family's health.

PSALM 85:6

"Will you not revive us again, that your people may rejoice in you?"

As you pray, we hope that the following outline will help you. Discuss these together so that you are praising and thanking focused on the truth of who God is and what He has done.

1. Praise God for who He is:

   Have each person share an attribute of God they are thankful for and why. Direct your conversation to God, as you praise Him, and rejoice in how He has revealed Himself to us.

2. Thank God for what He has done:
   - Begin with your *so great salvation*.
   - Thank Him for other good gifts He has given you.
   - Thank Him for the privilege of being able to be on mission for Him.

3. Requests you have as a group:
   - Pray for your children. If you don't have children, for the youth of our church, and any in your group that do have children. Also pray for parents who are seeking to disciple their children through these next stages.

4. For revival:

"7 Submit yourselves therefore to God. Resist the devil, and he will flee from you. 8 Draw near to God, and he will draw near to you. Cleanse your hands, you sinners, and purify your hearts, you double-minded." James 4:7–8

Open your hands and fully submit to God. Take the time to declare this.

You resist the devil by choosing obedience, take the time to quietly root out sin in your life, and commit to live for Jesus (repent).

Declare that you will be one who is seeking *single-minded* devotion to God.

MEMORIZE
& MEDITATE

"If we say we have no sin, we deceive ourselves, and the truth is not in us. [9] If we confess our sins, he is faithful and just to forgive us our sins and to cleanse us from all unrighteousness."

1 JOHN 1:8–9

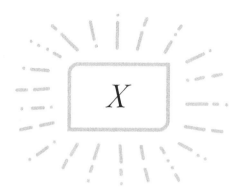

THE STRUGGLE: KEYSTONE HABITS

Romans 1–7 / Jude 17–25

The book of Romans has taken us from the glories of the Gospel to the struggles in obedience. This journey is one that every authentic believer experiences, and perhaps is experiencing today. The struggle is one of a passionate pursuit of holiness, longing to be conformed to the image of Jesus, all the while knowing we are not.

In fact, heartbreakingly, the closer we get to Jesus the further away we realize we are. So how can we pursue holiness, in the midst of this kind of brokenness without despair. The answer *build ourselves up in our most holy faith*. In this case, do so with keystone habits, and become more and more who Jesus wants us to be as we live our lives to the praise of His glorious grace.

Our goal in this message is to discover the pathway to growth, and *get on it*, and *stay on it*. Join us in this journey, and as we shine a light on helpful habits, begin to develop these in your life.

THE STRUGGLE: KEYSTONE HABITS

ROMANS 1–7 / JUDE 17–25

Introduction

1. Passion for perfection

- Follow God's Word or fake it

- Live in community or cause division

2. Dependence or destruction

PHILIPPIANS 2:12–13   PSALM 127:1   JOHN 15:5

3. Keystone habits engaged

1 TIMOTHY 4:8

Intake God's Word
- John 17:17
- Psalm 119:11
- Joshua 1:8
- Colossians 3:16–17

Invest in prayer
- Luke 18:1
- Colossians 4:2
- John 15
- Ephesians 6:18
- 1 Thessalonians 5:17–18
- Luke 22:39

Intentional community
- Hebrews 3:12–15
- Hebrews 10:24–25

Internalize the glories of the gospel every day
- Freedom: Romans 8:1
- Passion: 2 Corinthians 5:14
- Love: Romans 5:8; 1 John 4:19; Ephesians 5:1–2
- Forgiveness: Matthew 18:21–35; Ephesians 4:32
- Identity: 2 Corinthians 5:21
- Humility: Matthew 5:3
- Passion for lost souls: 2 Corinthians 5:18–21
- Joy: 1 Peter 1:8

EXTRA NOTES

EXTRA NOTES

GROWTH GROUP QUESTIONS

ROMANS 1–7 / JUDE 17–25

- How can we pursue holiness in a strategic manner?

- Why should we be seeking to obey Jesus in every area of our lives?

- In your life, when have you seen the most significant growth towards Jesus?

- Why does Jude take the time to show us that there are fake disciples, and that these disciples don't follow Jesus they just do what they want?

- Why is pursuing unity used by Jude as a key entry point to building ourselves up in our most holy faith?

- Why do you think that God hates those who cause division?
  PROVERBS 6:16–19

- What are ways we can pursue unity, and stop those around us who would create division?

- How can we pursue excellence in humility, without thinking we are creating division?

- What is a *keystone* habit?

- Discuss the four *keystone* habits for the growing Christian in a way that shows you understand what they are, and how you can apply them?

  > Intake God's Word

  > Invest in prayer

  > Intentional community

  > Internalize the glories of the gospel

- Can you as a group think of any creative ways that we can pursue these as a church family?

- What commitments are you willing to make to *"build yourself up in your most holy faith"*?

EXTRA NOTES

EXTRA NOTES

PRAYER

Thank you for praying together as a small group. We believe that prayer together is essential to your health and our family's health.

> ### PSALM 85:6

"Will you not revive us again, that your people may rejoice in you?"

As you pray, we hope that the following outline will help you. Discuss these together so that you are praising and thanking focused on the truth of who God is and what He has done.

1. Praise God for who He is:

   Have each person share an attribute of God they are thankful for and why. Direct your conversation to God, as you praise Him, and rejoice in how He has revealed Himself to us.

2. Thank God for what He has done:

   • Begin with your *so great salvation*

   • Thank Him for other good gifts He has given you

   • Thank Him for the privilege of being able to be on mission for Him

3. Requests you have as a group:

   • Pray for your children. If you don't have children, for the youth of our church, and any in your group that do have children. Also pray for parents who are seeking to disciple their children through these next stages.

4. For revival:

"7 Submit yourselves therefore to God. Resist the devil, and he will flee from you. 8 Draw near to God, and he will draw near to you. Cleanse your hands, you sinners, and purify your hearts, you double-minded." James 4:7–8

Open your hands and fully submit to God. Take the time to declare this.

You resist the devil by choosing obedience, take the time to quietly root out sin in your life, and commit to live for Jesus (repent).

Declare that you will be one who is seeking *single-minded* devotion to God.

MEMORIZE
& MEDITATE

"But you, beloved, building yourselves up in your most holy faith and praying in the Holy Spirit."

JUDE 20

"For while bodily training is of some value, godliness is of value in every way, as it holds promise for the present life and also for the life to come."

1 TIMOTHY 4:8

ADDITIONAL ARTICLES

WHAT IS THE GOSPEL?

We often talk about being Gospel-centred or Gospel-focused. To understand how to build a culture that is honouring to God, it is essential that we understand, experience, and constantly bathe in the Gospel. To begin growth in being a Gospel-centred culture, we must grasp what the Gospel is. There are many in our world who use the term but don't understand or experience the transformation.

The Gospel is literally *"the good news,"* and it is good because it addresses the deepest and most desperate need that all humans have. The Bible is clear that getting the Gospel wrong is dangerous (Galatians 1:8–10) and leads to destruction. It is very sad that there are those who think they are saved but are not (Matthew 7:21–27) and those who are saved by grace through faith who are not living in the fullness of what experiencing the Gospel daily provides.

To experience this good news there are five realities that must be grasped, believed, and then lived in light of daily experience.

1. God: A rich experience of the gospel is God-centred and always includes a belief about who God is that matches how He has revealed Himself in His Word. There is only one true God, who is holy, who made us in His image to worship Him. His holiness refers to His separateness from His creation and His absolute purity.

2. Humans: All humans have sinned (Romans 3:23) and in this have separated ourselves from God and are placed us under His righteous wrath. The wages of sin is death (Romans 6:23), and the only way for sinners to pay for sin is to spend eternity separated from God in hell.

3. Jesus: God loved us so much that He, according to His eternal plan, sent Jesus, His only Son into the world. Jesus lived a perfect life thus fulfilling the law Himself in our place; He died on the cross in our place thus taking on Himself the sins of those who believe in Him. He rose again from the dead and in this conquered sin and death. This displayed that God accepted His sacrifice, and that God's wrath against sinners who believe in Jesus has been fully exhausted.

4. Humans: God now calls on humans, by grace through faith, to repent of their sins and trust in Jesus alone for forgiveness. This belief in Jesus alone is a faith that saves. When humans believe they are forgiven and reconciled to God, this new relationship becomes the centre of their lives.

5. Spirit-Filled Life: All who are saved by grace through faith are made new creations, and seek to live a life that is surrendered to the Lordship of Jesus and devoted to His glory. This pursuit of holiness is a progression that He helps believers to pursue. The Spirit-filled life will include a desire to never ignore so great a salvation.

Mark Dever summarizes it like this...

A good way to summarize this good news is to biblically unpack the words God, Man, Christ, Response.

1. God: God is the creator of all things (Gen. 1:1). He is perfectly holy, worthy of all worship, and will punish sin (1 John 1:5, Rev. 4:11, Rom. 2:5–8).

2. Man: All people, though created good, have become sinful by nature (Gen. 1:26–28, Ps. 51:5, Rom. 3:23). From birth, all people are alienated from God, hostile to God, and subject to the wrath of God (Eph. 2:1–3).

3. Christ: Jesus Christ, who is fully God and fully man, lived a sinless life, died on the cross to bear God's wrath in the place of all who would believe in him, and rose from the grave in order to give his people eternal life (John 1:1, 1 Tim. 2:5, Heb. 7:26, Rom. 3:21–26, 2 Cor. 5:21, 1 Cor. 15:20–22).

4. Response: God calls everyone everywhere to repent of their sins and trust in Christ in order to be saved (Mark 1:15, Acts 20:21, Rom. 10:9–10).

(Some of this material has been adapted from The Gospel and Personal Evangelism by Mark Dever, p. 43)

https://www.9marks.org/answer/what-gospel/

The Gospel is so simple that a child can understand it, and yet so profound, that it will be something those who know Jesus will spend eternity celebrating (Ephesians 2:7).

These realities of the Gospel are amazing and must be grasped, believed, and experienced to be saved and to live a victorious Christian life. It is not enough to know them, or even to believe them—they ***must never be neglected*** (Heb 2:3). The best way to "escape" this danger is to preach the Gospel to ourselves every day.

KEEPING THE GOSPEL IN YOUR TESTIMONY

Q: Are we supposed to be able to share our faith?

A: 1 Peter 3:15–16: *"But in your hearts set apart Christ as Lord. Always be prepared to give an answer to everyone who asks you to give the reason for the hope that you have. But do this with gentleness and respect, keeping a clear conscience, so that those who speak maliciously against your good behavior in Christ may be ashamed of their slander."*

Q: Is the gospel an important part of this sharing? Can we just talk about how we helped ourselves, or our Grandma helped us, or our friend, or our auto-mechanic, or, or, or...

A: 2 Corinthians 4:5: *"For we do not preach ourselves, but Jesus Christ as Lord..."*

1 Corinthians 1:23: *"But we preach Christ crucified: a stumbling block to Jews and foolishness to Gentiles."*

Q: How can I structure my testimony?

A straightforward way to structure your testimony is in three stages:

Before: Simply tell what your life was like before you surrendered to Christ. What were you searching for before coming to know Christ? What was the key problem, emotion, situation or attitude you were dealing with? What motivated you? What were your actions? How did you try to satisfy your inner needs? (Examples of inner needs are loneliness, fear of death, insecurity. Possible ways to fill those needs include work, money, drugs, relationships, sports, sex.)

How: How were you converted? Simply tell the events and circumstances that caused you to consider Christ as the solution to your searching. Take time to identify the steps that brought you to the point of trusting Christ. Where were you? What was happening at the time? What people or problems influenced your decision?

Since: How has your life in Christ made a difference? How has his forgiveness impacted you? How have your thoughts, attitudes and emotions changed? Share how Christ is meeting your needs and what a relationship with him means to you now.

IMPORTANT TIPS TO REMEMBER

- **Stick to the point.** Your conversion and new life in Christ should be the main points.

- **Be specific.** Include events, genuine feelings and personal insights that clarify your main point. This makes your testimony tangible—something others can relate to.

- **Be current.** Tell what is happening in your life with God now, today.

- **Be honest.** Don't exaggerate or dramatize your life for effect. The simple truth of what God has done in your life is all the Holy Spirit needs to convict others of their sin and convince them of his love and grace.

Things to avoid:

Stay away from *"Christianese"* phrases. These *"foreign"* or *"churchy"* words can alienate listeners and readers and keep them from identifying with your life.

COMPONENTS OF THE GOSPEL TO INCLUDE IN YOUR TESTIMONY

Based on the colours of the bracelet.

Yellow

The first colour on our bracelet is yellow. What does yellow symbolize? Heaven. God's Home. This is where we should all want to go, and it is where we can go if we are in right relationship with God. This is by grace, through faith, resulting in obedience.

Focus on God and His *holiness* (God has no sin and is morally perfect, and set apart from everyone else. There is no one like Him!) Heaven is a place to rightly want to go...The gospel is God-centred!

Black

But—we have one problem. That is we have sin in our lives. The black colour represents our sin. The Bible says that all of us have sin. Romans 3:23, *"For all have sinned and come short of the glory of God."* God does not allow any sin in heaven. So how can we get into heaven? We can't. God says the punishment of sin is death. Death is eternal separation from God in hell.

Romans 6:23 *"For the wages of sin is death."*

At this point you want people to understand that they have done wrong things and that these wrong things have broken their relationship with God, and they can't earn their way back—ever.

Red

The red colour symbolizes Christ's blood. When we accept His free gift of salvation, God washes us with his blood. God sent his Son, Jesus Christ, to die on the cross in our place so that we don't have to receive the punishment we deserve for our sins! (*Grace*: It is important to talk about how this was something that we didn't deserve, and can't earn even in part.) To make our relationship with God right, what we have to do is believe in Jesus as our Lord and Savior, and accept what He did on the cross for us as a replacement for the punishment of sin. 2 Corinthians 5:21; Romans 10:9–10; Ephesians 2:8–10; John 3:16–17; Acts 4:12

When we really believe in Jesus as our Lord and Savior, this will include submission to God and learning to follow Him with our lives.

At this point you want the people to understand what it means to believe, and follow. Please focus on the person of Jesus and what He has done for us. Repentance summarizes this concept well—a change of mind that impacts every area of life, a change of direction.

White

Once Jesus washes us with His blood we are pure. We are no longer black with sin, but we are clean like the white colour. Because God took the place of our sin, when we die God can let us into heaven because our sin is paid for by Jesus' death on the cross. Romans 8:1; 1 Peter 2:24; John 1:12, 29; John 3:16

Green

After we believe in Jesus as our Lord and Savior, we want to grow so that we can become closer to God. The green symbolizes growth much like green grass. We can grow by reading the Bible, praying to God, going to church and learning to obey God in all of life (baptism and beyond).

Jude 1:20 *"But you dear friends build yourselves up in your most holy faith and pray in the Holy Spirit."*

* * *

PASTOR LES' TESTIMONY

Before Conversion

I was born in Calgary, Alberta, to parents who at that time, felt they could not raise me, so at six weeks old I was adopted into the Harder family. I grew up in a family that brought us to church weekly and taught us about having a relationship with Jesus Christ. When I was 5, I remember asking my mom about Jesus and what it means to be a Christian. She explained to me that we are all sinners and need to ask Jesus to forgive us for all the sins we have committed. Then we needed to ask Jesus into our hearts so that we can allow him to live in our hearts. As a five-year-old, this was something that I felt I wanted in my life, so in the privacy of my bedroom I ask Jesus into my heart.

As a five-year-old, I'm sure I didn't fully understand what it meant to live a life as a follower of Jesus Christ. As I grew up and navigated myself through my teens, God was working on my heart. I had a tough family life for many years as I watched my siblings walk away from God, and I watched my parents struggle to understand why things were going the way they were. So, my teen years were spent on things that satisfied my own fleshly desires (friends, hockey, girlfriend). But God never gave up on me and my soft heart towards Godly things. Throughout my teen years I re-dedicated my life back to God several times. I was a slow learner.

I was baptized at the age of 15. This played a huge part in my life. When you get baptized you are stating publicly that you want to live your life for Jesus for the rest of your life. This image of loyalty to Jesus and commitment being made for all to see has always served as a reminder for me to stay true to the Word of God and the relationship that I have with Him. Even though I have stumbled, and I haven't always walked in a right relationship with God, He has always drawn me back to His side and it has always stuck in my head that I declared publicly that I wanted to be a Christian.

After I met my wife DeeDee and we were married and having children at the age of 21, God really took hold of my life and revealed himself through his Son Jesus and what he had done for me on the cross. I had a man in my life at that time who really took the time to explain the reality of living your life for Jesus. It was then that I truly gave my life to God as a follower of Jesus Christ. From that point on I knew that I needed to live my life as a TRUE follower of Jesus.

Since that day my desire has always been to serve God and to show by example to my wife and family what it means to live in a relationship with Jesus.

After Conversion

Since I gave my life to the Lord completely, God has been shaping me, molding me and growing me in my relationship with Him. I started to serve God through the body of Christ in the local church. My desire was to let anyone I encountered know that I was a follower of Jesus. Whether that was at work, on the ice in an arena, or mentoring my kids and family members. I got myself involved in the church by serving on Deacon boards, serving on worship teams and leading Sunday morning services and of course I was totally committed to serving as a leader in youth ministries.

I've always had a desire to work in a church and always wanted to be a pastor, but I never thought in a million years that God would give me the desires of my heart. I used to pray that God would take me and use me for his glory. I started my working years in the Mills working as a laborer, I moved from that and became a trucker all the while serving Jesus in the local church, but I could never get it out of my head that I wanted to be a Pastor. In the year 2001 God called me to be a Pastor. DeeDee and I gave up all we had, our house, my trucking business, our cars, we gave up everything we owned and by faith moved back to Salmon Arm and started an internship with a Pastor in Salmon Arm. I took a few theology courses, I studied the Bible and learned as a student on the ground working in full time ministry. When I was 33 years old, God gave me my first Pastorate as a youth Pastor in Houston BC. I moved from there back to Salmon Arm where I spent 10 years as a youth Pastor and then a Campus Pastor of the Shuswap Community Church in Sorrento. I have seen God's provision and His love and care for me in my life as I've grown to love and serve him over the past 15 years. God has provided for me and my family in so many ways. He has taken the experiences I've had as a Pastor and grown me in my walk and relationship with Him.

All this brought me to this time in my life where I watched God take what I thought to be an impossible situation and again He gave me the desires of my heart which was always to be a Worship Pastor leading God's people through scripture, prayer and song. Throughout my life, I've learned that I can always trust God to lead and guide me. I know without a doubt in my mind that God has me in the place He has called me to. I know that I must serve and follow God, that I can trust him with my life and that He has my best interest in mind. I praise God that He has chosen me to be a child of God.

●   ●   ●

KEY STONE HABITS

There are very few things that you can learn or do that actually can have an everyday impact. Most knowledge that you gain builds on itself, and the accumulative growth brings change. It is not the individual things that you learn at school that make the most difference (okay a few big ones), rather the ability to learn and the growth of knowledge as a whole. There are however a few lessons that, when learned, can actually impact everything else. For children, learning to crawl and then walk (perhaps as important going to the bathroom on their own), speaking then reading, all makes the world a much bigger place.

In the Christian walk there are some essential world changing things to know, however the constant growth is also essential. The great thing about Christianity is even those things that are essential at the start can fascinate for the rest of eternity: how great God is, how profound His love, the wonder of His wisdom and power searching the depth of His character will only grow better as we grow older. We should know the Gospel and how to share it. We should know God's holiness and love and how they explode at the cross and then rejoice in it. There is so much to know and grow in, that sometimes it can feel overwhelming. So where do we begin. How do we continue?

There are some keystone habits for the Christian that are essential for the overall walk, for learning to know God better and living in obedience to His Word. They are habits that Influence all of life, even as they develop in their own specific impact area.

A *keystone habit* is a habit that develops a number of other good habits, and produces not only the positive impact related to that particular habit, but over-flows into many other areas of life. Keystone habits are *key* to becoming a healthy Christian, and for learning to build yourself up in your most holy faith.

For the Christian there are four keystone habits that will shape your intimacy with Jesus and impact on mission for Him in the church and the world. The overflow of their influence will change the trajectory of your entire life if you're willing to put the effort in to making them a part of the pattern of your life.

1. Preach
2. Pursue
3. Pray
4. People

KEYSTONE HABIT #1: PREACH

Preach the gospel to yourself everyday

This is a lesson that Jerry Bridges taught me very early on in my walk with God, and one that has impacted me perhaps more than any other. Of all of the keystone habits this is the most important, and perhaps the most impactful.

The Gospel of Jesus is not only the entry point to a reconciled relationship with God, it is the key to joyful victory in everyday living. It is practicing the discipline of reminding oneself of the richness of what Jesus has done on the cross, so that the reality of our own sin, and the battle we still have with the world the flesh and the devil can be done with full confidence, and engaged in with overflowing passion.

Jesus gave the church two habits: one at the entry point into relationship with Him, and the other as an ongoing reminder communion and baptism display the importance of this action for all followers of Jesus.

The Gospel serves as the very center of a heart that is fully devoted to Jesus. It motivates the follower of Jesus to obey (Hebrews 2:3) and be people who do not ignore so great a salvation! The Gospel compels Jesus followers to a life of full devotion to their Master (2 Corinthians 5:14; Romans 12:1–2) and if we are having trouble in our spiritual life it is always related foundationally to our experience of the Gospel. It serves to inflame the heart, deepen the devotion, and keep the servant on track when life isn't yielding desired results. It is the starting and staying place for every faithful follower of Jesus.

Colossians 1:4–6 states, *"⁴ since we heard of your faith in Christ Jesus and of the love that you have for all the saints, ⁵ because of the hope laid up for you in heaven. Of this you have heard before in the word of the truth, the gospel, ⁶ which has come to you, as indeed in the whole world it is bearing fruit and increasing—as it also does among you, since the day you heard it and understood the grace of God in truth,"*

The Gospel here is described as bearing fruit and increasing. It is not just content to be known and believed but also to be experienced and deepened. The Gospel not only introduces disciples to God, it also produces the motives and freedoms that come from its work in their lives. There is so much that comes from a proper experience of the Gospel:

- **Freedom:** Romans 8:1
- **Passion:** 2 Corinthians 5:14
- **Love:** Romans 5:8; 1 John 4:19; Ephesians 5:1–2
- **Forgiveness:** Matthew 18:21–35; Ephesians 4:32
- **Identity:** 2 Corinthians 5:21
- **Humility:** Matthew 5:3
- **Passion for Mission:** 2 Corinthians 5:18–21
- **Joy:** 1 Peter 1:8

If you live your life in the context of what Jesus has done for you, you will never be the same, and every other area of life is impacted.

How do disciples remind themselves of the Gospel every day so that it can be applied to every area of their thinking, believing and living?

It is the discipline of actively calling to mind what Jesus has done,
and the wonderful results of this gift of salvation,
and personalizing this relational reality.

It is acknowledging the fullness of the Gospel and then reminding oneself of the implications. This can be done standing in front of a mirror and talking to yourself (perhaps when no one else is around), or in prayer, rejoicing in who God is and what He has done.

It is a great place to begin your day, with a song, or hymn, or spiritual song. I love to wake up to the song, *Jesus Thank You*, a Sovereign Grace song written by a friend, it begins my day with the joy of knowing what Jesus did for me, and almost always it is reflected in my heartfelt joy.

Preaching the Gospel to yourself is also great as a weapon against condemnation and apathy, against pride and self-pity, and the list could go on. It is the antidote to much sin, and the pathway to overflowing overwhelming joy. When you are tempted to feel overcome in guilt and shame at your sin, remind yourself that Jesus' life, death and resurrection are what give you forgiveness and freedom. Memorize important Scriptures like Romans 8:1, or 1 John 1:9, and live in light of this reality, and when you are not experiencing the richness that comes from the Gospel, stop and fix your eyes on Jesus.

If you are tempted to pride, or self-pity, remind yourself of Ephesians 2:8–10, and rejoice in God's workmanship, He gets the glory and you have immense value in Him. Boast in your weaknesses, and remember that God uses weak people (1 Corinthians 1:18–30; 2 Corinthians 12:9–10).

If you lack passion and find yourself apathetic, meditate on the love of Jesus as seen in the cross, and you will find yourself compelled (2 Corinthians 5:14). You will be like a tube of toothpaste being squeezed as God's love presses in on your heart it produces joy filled obedience and confident service.

It is not a surprise that the ordinances God has given the church focus on this reality, remembering, fixing our eyes on Jesus, proclaiming His death until He returns, rejoicing in our identity in Him. The habit of living constantly in the presence of the reality of the work of Christ on the cross is a discipline that will change your entire life.

The Gospel must be central in our thoughts and lives if we are to live confident, obedient, joy filled lives.

It is the discipline of actively calling to mind what Jesus has done for you, and the wonderful results of this gift of salvation, and personalizing this relational reality.

When I am praying, I journal, and in this I seek to thank God early on for what He has done for me in the Gospel and plead with Him to deepen my experience of His love (Ephesians 3:14–21). Consciously place the beauty of your salvation before your eyes every day!

Preach the gospel to yourself every day!

Making the habit happen:
In your own words, what does it mean to preach the Gospel to yourself every day?

What are some disciplines you will build into your life so that you develop this keystone habit?

I am committed to preaching the Gospel to myself every day, and will do these three things to make this happen:

1.

2.

3.

Signed: _____

KEYSTONE HABIT #2: PURSUE

Pursue Word-saturation

The second most important relational keystone habit is the consistent pursuit of word-saturation—longing to know God's Word and live in light of it.

Charles Spurgeon understood this well when he wrote:

"Oh, that you and I might get into the very heart of the Word of God, and get that Word into ourselves! As I have seen the silkworm eat into the leaf, and consume it, so ought we to do with the Word of the Lord—not crawl over its surface, but eat right into it till we have taken it into our inmost parts. It is idle merely to let the eye glance over the words, or to recollect the poetical expressions, or the historic facts; but it is blessed to eat into the very soul of the Bible until, at last, you come to talk in Scriptural language, and your very style is fashioned upon Scripture models, and, what is better still, your spirit is flavored with the words of the Lord."

I would quote John Bunyan as an instance of what I mean. Read anything of his, and you will see that it is almost like the reading the Bible itself. He had read it till his very soul was saturated with Scripture; and, though his writings are charmingly full of poetry, yet he cannot give us his Pilgrim's Progress—that sweetest of all prose poems—without continually making us feel and say, *"why, this man is a living Bible!"* Prick him anywhere—his blood is Bibline, the very essence of the Bible flows from him. He cannot speak without quoting a text, for his very soul is full of the Word of God. I commend his example to you, beloved.

—*"Mr. Spurgeon as a Literary Man"* in The Autobiography of Charles H. Spurgeon, Compiled from His Letters, Diaries, and Records by His Wife and Private Secretary, vol. 4, 1878–1892 (Curtis & Jennings, 1900), p. 268.

Jesus' high priestly prayer shows us the importance of God's Word to our continual growth. *"Sanctify them by the truth, your word is truth"* (John 17:17). Help them to become holy, and use your Word to do it, so the Bible becomes our best friend in our pursuit of holiness. The center of the Bible is a Psalm that shows the incredible value of the Bible, *"I have stored up your word in my heart, that I might not sin against you"* (Psalm 119:11). It is well worth the time to read through Psalm 119 and see how God uses His Word to shape His people.

Most importantly, the Word reveals to us who God is, and it is only through Spirit filled study of His Word that we can actually get to know Him. The value of God's Word is surpassed (Psalm 138:2; Psalm 19) only by His Name, and in fact is the only way we can know His Name.

Psalm 138:2 declares, *"I bow down toward your holy temple and give thanks to your name for your steadfast love and your faithfulness, for you have exalted above all things your name and your word."* In fact in the Hebrew it is even stronger than this, *"you have exalted above your name, your word."* What God is communicating here is the value of His Word on display in its main priority of deepening our understanding of the name (character) of God so that we can know Him and make Him known. God's Word becomes our pathway into the presence of God, and helps us to evaluate everything we think about God and life.

Colossians 3:16–17 16 *"Let the word of Christ dwell in you richly, teaching and admonishing one another in all wisdom, singing psalms and hymns and spiritual songs, with thankfulness in your hearts to God. 17 And whatever you do, in word or deed, do everything in the name of the Lord Jesus, giving thanks to God the Father through him."*

This dwelling of God's Word in His followers is the key to victory over sin and delight in the Savior. God's Word is His revealing of Himself, His ways with mankind and how we can know Him and live for His glory. It is not only essential to read to grow in our intimacy with Him, but also to grow in our conformity to Him.

Romans 12:1–21 *"I appeal to you therefore, brothers,a by the mercies of God, to present your bodies as a living sacrifice, holy and acceptable to God, which is your spiritual worship. 2Do not be conformed to this world, but be transformed by the renewal of your mind, that by testing you may discern what is the will of God, what is good and acceptable and perfect."*

Followers of Jesus need this renewal or they will find themselves coasting downhill in the worldliness pattern. It is a choice between being Word-saturated or worldly wanderers. God's Word is inspired, inerrant and sufficient, and as such God's people must saturate themselves in it from Genesis to Revelation.

So how do disciples grow in their Word-saturation?

READ

This seems pretty simple, and yet needs to be stated, if you want to be Word saturated you must spend time reading God's Word. This should be done daily, and should cover the entire Bible. It is my belief that every Christian should be reading through the Bible and, at least once every two years, have read the Bible cover to cover. Not only this, an emphasis should be made on reading passages that are especially meaningful for your life now. These will be brought to you with the help of the Holy Spirit, and other believers, and can be lived in so that the memory that is filled with God's Word is constantly growing.

There are many who have moved away from reading, and this is a tragedy. It is not that you can't listen to God's Word and benefit from this time, but God's Word should be read and responded to. Make this a habit so that you can honestly say that God's Word is dwelling in you!

LISTEN

Listen to God's Word faithfully being preached. By this I actually mean find a church that preaches God's Word and commit yourself to her (more on this later). When you are committed to listening to expository preaching in community it will strengthen the depth of your knowledge of God's Word.

As your preacher works through books and the content of the sermon is driven by the content of the text you, will grow deeper and wider. There are many reasons to choose a church—the main one is the faithful preaching of God's Word and the impact this will have on you and others around you.

Take the time to prepare to listen, so that your heart is ready to respond to God's Word. Read the passage beforehand, give some thought to what you think it means and how it can apply to your life and when the sermon is preached, actively listen with open Bible and pen in hand.

STUDY

Studying God's Word is done when you try to take a smaller portion of Scripture and seek to understand how it fits into the whole and what it is saying at a deeper level. You can study in groups, or on your own and there are many study helps available online and in books and commentaries. It is taking the time to purposely go under the surface, to place things in their context and to understand what the text means at another level.

Remember when it comes to God's Word, it is truth, and we are sanctified as we know the truth, deeper and wider.

MEDITATE AND MEMORIZE

To meditate is to chew on and think through, to memorize is to think on and don't let go. As we hide God's Word in our hearts we are able to find victory in our battle against sin (Psalm 119:11). God's Word is the key weapon in our fight for holiness (John 17:17), and memorizing and meditating provide the pathway to Word saturation. Psalm 1 introduces a pathway to victory and it includes meditating on the Law of God day and night.

Choose a few passages that are precious, Romans 8 or John 15 are good starting places but there are so many more, and write a few verses out on cue cards and then think about them often, review them often, and don't stop. Choose the verse of the month from CBC as another great starting place for memorizing. Challenge your family or friends, and in grace pursue that one verse a month goal of getting God's Word into your heart. Join A.W.A.N.A. as a listener, and eventually all of the children saying their verses to you will give you an wealth of Scripture that rejoices your soul.

SHARE

This is where you share in humility what you are learning with others. The caution here is that you are inviting others of like passion to stand with you under the Word, so in that sense of tenderness of heart share what you are learning, how you are growing, what truths are transforming your heart. We are called to encourage one another daily, and the chief way that we do this is with God's Word flowing through our lives and lips (Hebrews 3:12–14).

LIVE IT!

Matthew 7:21–27 introduces the reality to the believer that we must not only know God's Word, we must live it. In fact applying God's Word to life is the key to a dynamic growing relationship with Him. To believe in Him as LORD is to be one who pursues active submission to His Word in all of life!

Look for ways you can know God better, and allow this knowledge to overflow into all of life! Be one God esteems, tremble at His Word (Isaiah 66:2), and become Word-saturated.

Pursue Word-saturation

I will read through the Bible in the coming year: _____

I will actively prepare my heart to receive from God's Word preached faithfully:

_____

I will memorize at least one verse a month, and seek to think about this verse in my coasting mind time: _____

I will seek to apply God's Word to my life, so that I am living in a relationship with Jesus that drives and defines me: _____

●   ●   ●

KEYSTONE HABIT #3: PRAYER

Prayer is communicating with God. We listen to Him when we read His Word, we speak to Him when we pray.

We are to be people who display our desperate dependence and His glorious faithfulness by praising His name, and brining to Him every request in thanksgiving. Jesus wants His followers to *always pray* and not give up (Luke 18:1). He wants us to know our dependence (Exodus 17:12–14), and live it out by choosing to communicate with Him in our times of need (Hebrews 4:16).

Prayer is the overflow of a heart that is living in relationship with God, and it is the practice of casting all of our anxieties on Him (1 Peter 5:7), or bringing to Him all of our anxieties. He wants to hear from us and is looking to strengthen those who are fully devoted to Him (2 Chronicles 16:9).

When should you pray? All of the time, or for extended periods of time? *Yes*! Nehemiah models this beautifully when he cries out to God for help for the people of Israel for an extended period of time, and then before the king shoots up an arrow prayer pleading with him for help in the moment. We should do both.

We should actively live in His presence, and constantly take everything to Him (1 Thessalonians 5:16–18) all the time (Psalm 16:8). God has chosen to use His people's prayers to accomplish His will. The most you can do for someone is to pray for them, after that, there are many things you can also do, but our relationship with God should be displayed in our prayer life. We know that unless the LORD builds the church, we are labouring in vain (Psalm 127:1). We know that apart from Him we can do nothing (John 15:1–11), and so we *pray*!

How should you pray? Well the simple answer is that there are all sorts of ways to pray (Ephesians 6:18), and we must be very careful to choose only one way to pray. We can learn from Jesus (Matthew 6) or the prayers of Biblical characters how to pray Biblically if we want to rightly pattern our prayers after what the Holy Spirit has inspired. Praying the Psalms, as Donald Whitney helpfully teaches, can also be a huge blessing and benefit as you learn and grow in pouring out of your heart to God His way. Don't worry about your words as much as guarding your heart (Proverbs 4:16) and allow the overflow of your heart to impact your words. Jesus does not need you to use thee's and thou's, although He does understand them—He wants to hear your heart overflowing and crying out to Him!

Why should you pray? Because it is commanded, and it is God's tool to grow you, and use you to impact others. It is relational and powerful (James 5:16) and something we should be growing deeper in all of the time as we know God more.

When should I start this Keystone Habit? Now!

Prayer: crying out to God

Today I commit to put reminders into my life that will help me actively be conscious of His presence:

Signed: _____

Reminders:

Today I will commit to bring things on my heart to God in prayer

Signed: _____

Today I will seek to add 5 minutes to my current pattern of extended prayer. If you don't pray at all, pray 5 minutes a day. If you pray now, add 5.

Signed: _____

If you have trouble knowing what to pray, you can follow Biblical prayers, pray through Psalms, or follow helpful acrostics...

A.C.T.S.

Adoration: Praise God for who He is

Confession: agree with God and his view of sin & rejoice in His forgiveness

Thanksgiving: Thank Him for what He has done for you on the cross, and His everyday gifts.

Supplication: This is the requests time—pour out every request on your mind.

I have been asked if there are prayer requests that are too small to bring to God, and the answer is either *of course*, they are all too small, or the right response, if it is on your heart, bring it to Him and you will experience His grace and love and He will use your prayers to accomplish His will and glorify His name!

Key things to pray for our congregation:

•L Love Relationship with God—core of who we are: Mark 12:28–31

That we would be a church that is relational and has an experience of God's love, to make a relationship which drives and defines everything else!

•O One heart and mind: Romans 15:5–6; Philippians 1:27

Unity together for God's Glory!

•V Vision would be God's and we will pursue together...HTML

- Philippians 1:21; Galatians 2:20
- 1 Peter 1:16
- John 17:17; 2 Timothy 3:16–17
- Matthew 28:16–20
- Ephesians 3:14–21; 1 Peter 4:8

•E Eager Servants: That we would be a great church full of eager servants.

Ephesians 4:11–16; John 13:1–14

Pray for God to bless us with numbers (a church full of people who are full of God) and commitment to Him as we seek His glory together.

Pray for a culture of evangelism and discipleship.

God will use our prayers to shape our pursuit of Him successfully together.

Helpful New Testaments prayers to pattern your own prayers after:

- Ephesians 1:17–19
- Ephesians 3:16–19
- Philippians 1:9–11
- Colossians 1:9–12
- 1 Thessalonians 3:9–13
- 2 Thessalonians 2:16–17
- 1 Timothy 2:1–4
- Romans 10:1

Memorize and meditate on: Colossians 4:2–4

● ● ●

KEYSTONE HABIT #4: PEOPLE

The healthy Christian will always live in community with the people of God in a local church. This keystone habit is a commitment not only to belong, and grow in a healthy church, but also to serve her and sacrificially help her to grow to be all that God wants her to be (Ephesians 4:11–16).

This is a habit that has been under attack from the forming of the church—perhaps because we are fallen people, perhaps because Satan hates what God loves, or perhaps because it is an easy thing to lose sight of in the busyness of the world.

God has chosen the church to be His change agent for the world. In the Bible, every individual Christian is seen as a part of a bigger family, commanded to take part in that family to give and receive and as a key part of the discipleship process.

If you are a part of the Church (you have believed the Gospel and joined God's family), you will be a part of a church (local church). This is not always easy as churches are filled with humans like you, but it is mandated, and the only way to be healthy as a Christian over the long term. There are no perfect churches, and if there were, you would wreck it when you joined, there are many imperfect churches that God is using His followers to beautify and if you are truly saved this is your mandate and privilege to be a part of.

Being committed to God's family means the following:

1. A commitment to community | HEBREWS 3:12–14; 10:24–25

The church is the place where we help one another grow towards Jesus. Without her, and our regular commitment to her we will not grow as God desires, and the deceitfulness of sin will steal our holiness and our joy and leave us empty and in despair.

We need one another to pursue holiness, and if we do not commit to this kind of community we will be in danger of developing hard hearts, and without knowingly choosing, moving on a pathway to sin. This commitment in our culture includes making Sunday a priority for the gathering of God's people and coming ready to hear from God's Word and serve, but also a desire to meet with smaller groups and build in opportunities to obey the *"one-another's"* of Scripture.

This first commitment is a time and priority commitment to make sure that in the busyness of life, the gathering of believers takes priority over almost everything else. For Canada and our current culture, this is Sunday morning, so this habit is to make Sunday morning a high priority that you pray for, prepare for even in your choices for Saturday night and in prayer.

2. A commitment to love & unity

You have heard it said, *"to dwell above with saints I love, oh wouldn't that be glory. But to live below with saints we know, well that's another story."*

Hmmm...not sure that is what we should be affirming, yet so often we do. I hear of struggles people had with the church, and of recent church historians who would say that many churches are on a 10 year division cycle.

Again, this is not surprising, as unity and love are repeatedly addressed in the New Testament as a goal we should pray for and pursue (Philippians 2; Romans 15:5–6, etc.). It is also interesting to be aware that the Bible outlines things God hates, including sowing *"discord among brothers"* (Proverbs 6:16–19).

So this commitment to the family of God, to God's people, is a commitment to selflessness and God centered love (Romans 12:10; Ephesians 5:1–2), a commitment to selflessly and courageously pursuing God's best. It is a commitment to avoid negativity and complaining and pursue self-sacrificial love and graciousness. In fact, in a healthy church when negativity is being shared, it is taken immediately to those who can deal with the issue, or dealt with as the sin of gossip or slander.

We are to be known for our love for one another, and in that, we need to Ephesians 4:32 one another. You need to forgive brothers and sisters in the church, or you will live with bitterness that will lead to the rejection of Jesus' bride and the removal of yourself from community, in brokenness. The cost is high if you don't make it your habit to choose love and unity over division and selfishness.

3. A commitment to God's Word

We have covered this already, but should restate that the priority of God's Word is the gathering of God's people in submission and praise.

Commit to a church that believes in expository preaching and as a friend once said, if God's Word is opened, you can always get something from the message regardless of the quality of the preacher.

Commit to active listening! To prepare your hearts on Saturday nights by reviewing the text, and spending time after the text was opened reviewing how it applies to your life. Take God's Word seriously and pursue active listening and responding to His Word in community!

4. A commitment to the gospel

This is and should remain the entrance point to the Church. However, also consider what we have already covered in the preaching of the Gospel to yourself every day.

The church is a place where the Gospel is displayed, not only through the ordinances, but also through the constant centrality of Jesus and His work. The mission of the church is to make disciples, and this mission includes guiding people into the Gospel and helping them to live in light of the Gospel in every area of their lives!

5. A commitment to service

The church is a place to belong, help others belong, and serve. It is only as each part does its work that the church will find unity and maturity (Eph. 4:11–16).

If you are someone who has believed in Jesus as your LORD and Savior, you must choose to serve His church, to build it up. If you are not serving it will stunt your growth, and you will be hurting the church you belong to. This means seeking to know your spiritual gift, and using it in His strength, for His glory (1 Peter 4:11–12).

6. A commitment to submission

This is hard in our world; however, it is important to remember. The church has God appointed leaders, and God calls His people to submit to them and make their ministry a joy (Hebrews 13:7, 17). This should be something that is easy, but from experience, it is probably not, as so often like the Israelites and Christians before us, we think we know better, feel better, or are more qualified. A part of following elders is choosing, on non-biblical issues, to submit fully even if you think they could have chosen a better path. Submission does not mean you don't talk, or share, or pursue what you think God's best is, but it always means you do so in a respectful manner that joins the team when the final decision is made.

That seems like a lot, so take the time to re-read this habit, and ask yourself if you are willing to make this a habit, or perhaps habits, that will yield growth.

Remember as you commit yourself to God's people that there is no perfect church, but God has chosen His people to be His change agent in the world. So commit to being a part of God's will in building her, and, in confidence, know He ultimately will build His church (Matthew 16:18).

I will seek to be a healthy member of a church, with all that entails: _____

I will seek to be one who God builds and be an encourager to those God places in my local family: _____

Take the time to re-read **Habit #4**, and look up the verses, as you seek to grow into who God wants you to become.

●   ●   ●

KEYSTONE HABIT #5: PREACH

Okay, we said only four, but this is a reminder to all of us, that if we are seeking to build into our lives these keystone habits we will not always succeed, so we need God's grace to overwhelm us with forgiveness and motivate us to full devotion.

Perhaps even more, if we are successful in these keystone habits, our intimacy with God will grow, and the more we grow and see Him for who He has revealed Himself to be, the more desperately we will need a clear and constant experience of the Gospel. So, don't forget—preach the Gospel to yourself every day!

Take 10 looks at Jesus for every one look at yourself, and see all of life through your relationship with Him.

Live in His presence

Jerry Bridges once shared that true revival comes from consciously living in His presence, as this gives power to live and purity in fleeing from sin. I think He is right, so practice Psalm 16:8, and live your life ever growing and glowing to the praise of His glorious grace.

Know that you can only work out your salvation as he works in you (Philippians 2:12–13) and that boasting in your weaknesses is a sought after quality as we know that in this the power of Christ will rest on us (2 Corinthians 12:10).

For humility, strength, and courage to go on, keep the Gospel central to your habit forming commitments, and if you fail (and you will), get up the next morning and begin again to form these habits that will shape so many others in your life.

In God's strength, for God's glory, these habits can become the foundation for your conformity to Christ, and with that foundation strong, the impact will reverberate not only in your life and through your life, but for all eternity.

●　　●　　●

34486536R00091

Made in the USA
Middletown, DE
27 January 2019